50 Healthy American Classic Recipes for Home

By: Kelly Johnson

Table of Contents

- Turkey Chili
- Grilled Chicken Salad
- Baked Sweet Potato Fries
- Whole Wheat Mac and Cheese
- Quinoa Stuffed Peppers
- Cauliflower Mashed Potatoes
- Turkey Meatloaf
- Veggie Burgers
- Black Bean Soup
- Grilled Salmon
- Zucchini Noodles with Marinara
- Chicken and Vegetable Stir-Fry
- Baked Chicken Tenders
- Lentil Sloppy Joes
- Baked Fish Tacos
- Sweet Potato and Black Bean Enchiladas
- Veggie Pizza on Whole Wheat Crust
- Grilled Portobello Mushrooms
- Whole Wheat Pancakes
- Greek Yogurt Parfaits
- Baked Apple Chips
- Turkey and Avocado Wraps
- Veggie Omelette
- Stuffed Acorn Squash
- Spinach and Feta Stuffed Chicken Breast
- Cauliflower Pizza Crust
- Kale and Quinoa Salad
- Broccoli Cheddar Soup (lightened)
- Shrimp and Veggie Skewers
- Brown Rice Risotto
- Oven-Baked Chicken Wings
- Spinach and Mushroom Quesadilla
- Roasted Brussels Sprouts
- Eggplant Parmesan (baked)
- Spaghetti Squash with Pesto

- Avocado Toast
- Hearty Vegetable Stew
- Banana Oatmeal Cookies
- Berry Smoothie Bowl
- Lemon Herb Grilled Chicken
- Chickpea Salad
- Roasted Beet Salad
- Stuffed Bell Peppers
- Carrot and Zucchini Muffins
- Hummus and Veggie Wrap
- Grilled Asparagus
- Tomato Basil Soup
- Chicken Caesar Salad (lightened)
- Sweet Potato and Kale Hash
- Blueberry Chia Pudding

Turkey Chili

Ingredients:

- 1 tablespoon olive oil
- 1 medium onion, diced
- 2 cloves garlic, minced
- 1 pound ground turkey
- 1 bell pepper, diced (any color)
- 1 jalapeño pepper, diced (optional, for added heat)
- 1 can (15 ounces) diced tomatoes
- 1 can (15 ounces) kidney beans, drained and rinsed
- 1 can (15 ounces) black beans, drained and rinsed
- 2 cups chicken or vegetable broth
- 2 tablespoons chili powder
- 1 teaspoon ground cumin
- 1 teaspoon paprika
- 1/2 teaspoon dried oregano
- Salt and pepper to taste
- Optional toppings: shredded cheese, diced avocado, chopped cilantro, sour cream

Instructions:

1. Sauté Aromatics: Heat the olive oil in a large pot over medium heat. Add the diced onion and cook for 3-4 minutes until softened. Add the minced garlic and cook for an additional 1 minute until fragrant.
2. Brown Turkey: Add the ground turkey to the pot, breaking it apart with a spoon, and cook until browned and no longer pink.
3. Add Peppers: Stir in the diced bell pepper and jalapeño pepper (if using) and cook for another 2-3 minutes until they begin to soften.
4. Combine Ingredients: Pour in the diced tomatoes, kidney beans, black beans, and chicken or vegetable broth. Stir in the chili powder, ground cumin, paprika, dried oregano, salt, and pepper.
5. Simmer: Bring the chili to a boil, then reduce the heat to low. Cover and simmer for 20-30 minutes, stirring occasionally, to allow the flavors to meld together and the chili to thicken to your desired consistency.
6. Serve: Ladle the turkey chili into bowls and top with your favorite toppings such as shredded cheese, diced avocado, chopped cilantro, or sour cream.
7. Enjoy: Serve the turkey chili hot and enjoy its hearty and comforting flavors!

This turkey chili is perfect for cozy nights in or for feeding a crowd at gatherings. It's also great for meal prep as it reheats well and can be frozen for later enjoyment.

Grilled Chicken Salad

Ingredients:

- 2 boneless, skinless chicken breasts
- Salt and pepper, to taste
- 1 tablespoon olive oil
- 6 cups mixed salad greens (such as lettuce, spinach, arugula)
- 1 cup cherry tomatoes, halved
- 1 cucumber, sliced
- 1/2 red onion, thinly sliced
- 1/4 cup sliced black olives
- 1/4 cup crumbled feta cheese (optional)
- Balsamic vinaigrette or your favorite salad dressing

Instructions:

1. Preheat Grill: Preheat your grill to medium-high heat.
2. Prepare Chicken: Season the chicken breasts with salt, pepper, and olive oil. Grill the chicken breasts for 6-8 minutes per side, or until they are cooked through and no longer pink in the center. Remove from the grill and let them rest for a few minutes before slicing.
3. Assemble Salad: In a large bowl, combine the mixed salad greens, cherry tomatoes, cucumber slices, red onion slices, and sliced black olives.
4. Slice Chicken: Slice the grilled chicken breasts into thin strips.
5. Serve: Divide the salad mixture onto plates or bowls. Top each portion with slices of grilled chicken. If desired, sprinkle crumbled feta cheese over the salads.
6. Dress: Drizzle the salads with your favorite salad dressing, such as balsamic vinaigrette or a lemon vinaigrette.
7. Enjoy: Serve the grilled chicken salad immediately and enjoy a light and refreshing meal!

This grilled chicken salad is not only healthy and nutritious but also packed with flavor. Feel free to customize the salad with your favorite vegetables or add additional toppings such as avocado, nuts, or seeds for extra crunch and texture.

Baked Sweet Potato Fries

Ingredients:

- 2 medium sweet potatoes, peeled and cut into fries
- 2 tablespoons olive oil
- 1 teaspoon paprika
- 1/2 teaspoon garlic powder
- 1/2 teaspoon onion powder
- 1/2 teaspoon ground cumin
- Salt and pepper, to taste
- Optional: chopped fresh parsley or cilantro for garnish

Instructions:

1. Preheat Oven: Preheat your oven to 425°F (220°C). Line a large baking sheet with parchment paper or aluminum foil for easy cleanup.
2. Prepare Sweet Potatoes: Place the sweet potato fries in a large bowl. Drizzle with olive oil and toss until evenly coated.
3. Season: In a small bowl, combine the paprika, garlic powder, onion powder, ground cumin, salt, and pepper. Sprinkle the seasoning mixture over the sweet potatoes and toss until evenly coated.
4. Arrange on Baking Sheet: Spread the seasoned sweet potato fries in a single layer on the prepared baking sheet, making sure they are not overcrowded.
5. Bake: Place the baking sheet in the preheated oven and bake for 20-25 minutes, flipping the fries halfway through, until the fries are crispy and golden brown.
6. Garnish and Serve: Remove the sweet potato fries from the oven and transfer them to a serving plate. If desired, garnish with chopped fresh parsley or cilantro. Serve hot and enjoy!

These baked sweet potato fries are a healthier alternative to traditional fries and make a tasty side dish or snack. They're crispy on the outside, tender on the inside, and packed with flavor from the seasonings.

Whole Wheat Mac and Cheese

Ingredients:

- 8 ounces whole wheat macaroni or pasta of your choice
- 2 tablespoons unsalted butter
- 2 tablespoons whole wheat flour
- 2 cups milk (preferably low-fat or skim)
- 2 cups shredded sharp cheddar cheese
- 1/2 teaspoon mustard powder
- Salt and pepper, to taste
- Optional toppings: breadcrumbs, chopped parsley, cooked bacon bits

Instructions:

1. Cook Pasta: Cook the whole wheat macaroni according to the package instructions until al dente. Drain and set aside.
2. Prepare Cheese Sauce: In a large saucepan, melt the butter over medium heat. Once melted, whisk in the whole wheat flour to form a roux. Cook the roux for 1-2 minutes until it turns a light golden color.
3. Add Milk: Gradually pour in the milk while whisking continuously to prevent lumps from forming. Cook the mixture, stirring frequently, until it thickens and comes to a simmer.
4. Add Cheese: Reduce the heat to low and stir in the shredded cheddar cheese, a little at a time, until it melts and the sauce is smooth and creamy. Stir in the mustard powder and season with salt and pepper to taste.
5. Combine Pasta and Sauce: Add the cooked whole wheat macaroni to the cheese sauce and stir until well coated and combined.
6. Serve: Transfer the whole wheat mac and cheese to serving bowls or a serving dish. If desired, sprinkle breadcrumbs, chopped parsley, or cooked bacon bits on top for added flavor and texture.
7. Enjoy: Serve the whole wheat mac and cheese hot and enjoy its creamy and cheesy goodness!

This whole wheat mac and cheese is a healthier twist on the classic comfort food dish, providing extra fiber and nutrients from the whole wheat pasta. It's perfect for a quick and satisfying meal that the whole family will love.

Quinoa Stuffed Peppers

Ingredients:

- 4 large bell peppers (any color), halved and seeds removed
- 1 cup quinoa, rinsed
- 2 cups vegetable broth or water
- 1 tablespoon olive oil
- 1 small onion, diced
- 2 cloves garlic, minced
- 1 medium zucchini, diced
- 1 medium carrot, grated
- 1 cup diced tomatoes (fresh or canned)
- 1 teaspoon dried oregano
- 1 teaspoon dried basil
- Salt and pepper, to taste
- 1 cup shredded cheese (such as cheddar or mozzarella), optional
- Fresh parsley or cilantro, chopped, for garnish

Instructions:

1. Preheat Oven: Preheat your oven to 375°F (190°C). Lightly grease a baking dish large enough to hold all of the pepper halves.
2. Cook Quinoa: In a medium saucepan, bring the vegetable broth or water to a boil. Add the quinoa, reduce the heat to low, cover, and simmer for 15-20 minutes, or until the quinoa is cooked and the liquid is absorbed. Remove from heat and fluff the quinoa with a fork.
3. Prepare Peppers: Place the halved bell peppers in the prepared baking dish, cut side up.
4. Sauté Vegetables: In a large skillet, heat the olive oil over medium heat. Add the diced onion and cook for 3-4 minutes until softened. Add the minced garlic and cook for an additional 1 minute until fragrant. Add the diced zucchini and grated carrot to the skillet and cook for 5-6 minutes until softened.
5. Combine Ingredients: Stir in the cooked quinoa, diced tomatoes, dried oregano, dried basil, salt, and pepper into the skillet with the cooked vegetables. Cook for an additional 2-3 minutes until heated through and well combined.
6. Stuff Peppers: Spoon the quinoa and vegetable mixture evenly into each bell pepper half, pressing down gently to pack the filling.
7. Bake: Cover the baking dish with aluminum foil and bake in the preheated oven for 25-30 minutes, or until the peppers are tender.

8. **Optional Cheese:** If using shredded cheese, remove the foil from the baking dish and sprinkle the cheese over the stuffed peppers during the last 5 minutes of baking. Return the dish to the oven until the cheese is melted and bubbly.
9. **Serve:** Remove the stuffed peppers from the oven and garnish with chopped fresh parsley or cilantro. Serve hot and enjoy!

These quinoa stuffed peppers are a nutritious and flavorful vegetarian dish that's perfect for a wholesome meal. They're packed with protein, fiber, and vitamins, making them a satisfying and healthy option for lunch or dinner.

Cauliflower Mashed Potatoes

Ingredients:

- 1 large head of cauliflower, chopped into florets
- 2 cloves garlic, minced
- 2 tablespoons unsalted butter or olive oil
- 1/4 cup milk (any kind, such as dairy milk or almond milk)
- Salt and pepper, to taste
- Optional toppings: chopped chives, grated Parmesan cheese

Instructions:

1. Steam Cauliflower: Place the cauliflower florets in a steamer basket set over a pot of boiling water. Cover and steam for 10-12 minutes, or until the cauliflower is very tender when pierced with a fork.
2. Drain and Dry: Remove the steamed cauliflower from the steamer basket and transfer it to a colander to drain excess moisture. Pat the cauliflower dry with paper towels to remove as much moisture as possible.
3. Mash Cauliflower: Transfer the drained cauliflower to a large bowl. Use a potato masher or fork to mash the cauliflower until it reaches your desired consistency. Alternatively, you can use a food processor for a smoother texture.
4. Sauté Garlic: In a small skillet, heat the butter or olive oil over medium heat. Add the minced garlic and cook for 1-2 minutes, stirring frequently, until fragrant but not browned.
5. Combine Ingredients: Pour the sautéed garlic and butter/oil mixture over the mashed cauliflower. Add the milk, salt, and pepper to taste. Stir until everything is well combined and the cauliflower is creamy.
6. Adjust Consistency: If the mashed cauliflower is too thick, you can add a little more milk until you reach your desired consistency.
7. Taste and Adjust Seasoning: Taste the cauliflower mashed potatoes and adjust the seasoning with more salt and pepper if needed.
8. Serve: Transfer the cauliflower mashed potatoes to a serving dish. If desired, sprinkle chopped chives or grated Parmesan cheese on top as a garnish.
9. Enjoy: Serve the cauliflower mashed potatoes hot as a delicious and nutritious side dish. They're perfect for serving alongside your favorite main courses!

These cauliflower mashed potatoes are creamy, flavorful, and low in carbohydrates, making them a great option for those looking to reduce their carb intake or add more vegetables to their diet.

Turkey Meatloaf

Ingredients:

- 1 lb ground turkey (preferably lean)
- 1/2 cup breadcrumbs (whole wheat or gluten-free)
- 1/4 cup milk (any kind, such as dairy milk or almond milk)
- 1 small onion, finely chopped
- 1 carrot, grated
- 1 celery stalk, finely chopped
- 2 cloves garlic, minced
- 1/4 cup ketchup (plus extra for topping)
- 1 tablespoon Worcestershire sauce
- 1 tablespoon Dijon mustard
- 1 teaspoon dried thyme
- 1 teaspoon dried oregano
- 1/2 teaspoon paprika
- Salt and pepper, to taste
- Optional: chopped fresh parsley for garnish

Instructions:

1. Preheat Oven: Preheat your oven to 375°F (190°C). Lightly grease a loaf pan or line it with parchment paper for easy cleanup.
2. Mix Ingredients: In a large mixing bowl, combine the ground turkey, breadcrumbs, milk, chopped onion, grated carrot, chopped celery, minced garlic, ketchup, Worcestershire sauce, Dijon mustard, dried thyme, dried oregano, paprika, salt, and pepper. Use your hands or a spoon to mix everything together until well combined.
3. Shape Loaf: Transfer the turkey mixture to the prepared loaf pan and shape it into a loaf shape, pressing it down gently to compact it.
4. Top with Ketchup: Spread a thin layer of ketchup over the top of the meatloaf for added flavor and moisture.
5. Bake: Place the loaf pan in the preheated oven and bake for 50-60 minutes, or until the meatloaf is cooked through and the top is golden brown. To check for doneness, insert a meat thermometer into the center of the meatloaf - it should register at least 165°F (75°C).
6. Rest: Once cooked, remove the meatloaf from the oven and let it rest in the pan for 5-10 minutes before slicing.

7. Slice and Serve: Slice the turkey meatloaf into thick slices and transfer them to serving plates. Garnish with chopped fresh parsley if desired.
8. Enjoy: Serve the turkey meatloaf hot with your favorite side dishes, such as mashed potatoes, steamed vegetables, or a green salad.

This turkey meatloaf is moist, flavorful, and easy to make, making it a perfect weeknight dinner option for the whole family. leftovers can be stored in the refrigerator for a few days or frozen for longer storage.

Veggie Burgers

Ingredients:

- 1 can (15 ounces) black beans, drained and rinsed
- 1 cup cooked quinoa
- 1/2 cup breadcrumbs (whole wheat or gluten-free)
- 1/4 cup finely chopped onion
- 1/4 cup finely chopped bell pepper (any color)
- 2 cloves garlic, minced
- 1 teaspoon ground cumin
- 1 teaspoon smoked paprika
- 1/2 teaspoon chili powder
- 1/4 teaspoon cayenne pepper (optional, for added heat)
- Salt and pepper, to taste
- 1 tablespoon olive oil (for cooking)

Optional toppings:

- Whole wheat burger buns
- Lettuce leaves
- Sliced tomato
- Sliced avocado
- Red onion slices
- Mustard or ketchup

Instructions:

1. Mash Beans: In a large mixing bowl, mash the black beans with a fork or potato masher until they are mostly mashed but still have some texture.
2. Add Ingredients: Add the cooked quinoa, breadcrumbs, chopped onion, chopped bell pepper, minced garlic, ground cumin, smoked paprika, chili powder, cayenne pepper (if using), salt, and pepper to the bowl with the mashed beans.
3. Mix: Use a spoon or your hands to mix all the ingredients together until well combined.
4. Form Patties: Divide the mixture into 4 equal portions. Shape each portion into a burger patty, pressing it firmly together to prevent it from falling apart during cooking. If the mixture feels too wet, you can add more breadcrumbs to help bind it together.

5. Cook Patties: Heat the olive oil in a large skillet over medium heat. Once hot, add the veggie burger patties to the skillet and cook for 4-5 minutes on each side, or until golden brown and crispy on the outside.
6. Serve: Once cooked through, remove the veggie burger patties from the skillet and transfer them to a serving plate. Serve the patties on whole wheat burger buns with your favorite toppings such as lettuce, tomato, avocado, and red onion slices. You can also add mustard or ketchup for extra flavor.
7. Enjoy: Serve the veggie burgers hot and enjoy their delicious and nutritious goodness!

These homemade veggie burgers are not only tasty and satisfying but also packed with protein, fiber, and vitamins from the beans, quinoa, and vegetables. They're perfect for a meatless meal option that the whole family will love.

Black Bean Soup

Ingredients:

- 2 cans (15 ounces each) black beans, drained and rinsed
- 1 tablespoon olive oil
- 1 onion, diced
- 2 cloves garlic, minced
- 1 bell pepper (any color), diced
- 1 jalapeño pepper, diced (optional, for added heat)
- 1 carrot, diced
- 1 celery stalk, diced
- 1 teaspoon ground cumin
- 1 teaspoon chili powder
- 1/2 teaspoon smoked paprika
- 4 cups vegetable broth
- 1 can (14.5 ounces) diced tomatoes
- Salt and pepper, to taste
- Juice of 1 lime
- Optional toppings: chopped fresh cilantro, diced avocado, sour cream or Greek yogurt, shredded cheese, tortilla strips

Instructions:

1. Sauté Aromatics: Heat the olive oil in a large pot or Dutch oven over medium heat. Add the diced onion and cook for 3-4 minutes until softened. Add the minced garlic, diced bell pepper, jalapeño pepper (if using), carrot, and celery. Cook for another 5-6 minutes until the vegetables are softened.
2. Add Spices: Stir in the ground cumin, chili powder, and smoked paprika. Cook for 1 minute until fragrant.
3. Simmer: Add the drained and rinsed black beans, vegetable broth, and diced tomatoes (with their juices) to the pot. Stir to combine. Bring the mixture to a simmer.
4. Blend (Optional): For a smoother consistency, you can use an immersion blender to partially blend the soup directly in the pot. Alternatively, transfer a portion of the soup to a blender and blend until smooth, then return it to the pot.
5. Season: Season the soup with salt and pepper to taste. Squeeze in the juice of 1 lime and stir to combine.
6. Simmer Further: Allow the soup to simmer for 15-20 minutes to allow the flavors to meld together and the soup to thicken slightly.

7. Serve: Ladle the black bean soup into serving bowls. Garnish with chopped fresh cilantro, diced avocado, a dollop of sour cream or Greek yogurt, shredded cheese, and tortilla strips, if desired.
8. Enjoy: Serve the black bean soup hot and enjoy its delicious and comforting flavors!

This black bean soup is perfect for a cozy weeknight dinner or as a meal prep option for quick and easy lunches throughout the week. It's vegetarian, vegan-friendly (if you skip the dairy toppings), and can be customized with your favorite toppings and spices.

Grilled Salmon

Ingredients:

- 4 salmon fillets, about 6 ounces each, skin-on or skinless
- 2 tablespoons olive oil
- 2 cloves garlic, minced
- 1 teaspoon lemon zest
- 1 tablespoon lemon juice
- 1 teaspoon dried dill (or 1 tablespoon chopped fresh dill)
- Salt and pepper, to taste
- Lemon wedges, for serving
- Fresh dill or parsley, chopped, for garnish

Instructions:

1. Prepare Salmon: Pat the salmon fillets dry with paper towels. If using skin-on salmon, lightly oil the skin side.
2. Marinade: In a small bowl, whisk together the olive oil, minced garlic, lemon zest, lemon juice, and dried dill. Season with salt and pepper to taste.
3. Marinate Salmon: Place the salmon fillets in a shallow dish or a resealable plastic bag. Pour the marinade over the salmon, making sure to coat each fillet evenly. Allow the salmon to marinate in the refrigerator for at least 30 minutes, or up to 2 hours.
4. Preheat Grill: Preheat your grill to medium-high heat. If using a charcoal grill, wait until the coals are hot and covered with ash.
5. Grill Salmon: Once the grill is hot, remove the salmon fillets from the marinade and shake off any excess. Place the salmon fillets on the grill, flesh side down. Close the lid and grill for 3-4 minutes.
6. Flip: Carefully flip the salmon fillets using a spatula. If the salmon has skin, you can gently peel it away from the grill grates if it sticks. Close the lid and continue grilling for an additional 3-4 minutes, or until the salmon is cooked through and flakes easily with a fork.
7. Serve: Remove the grilled salmon from the grill and transfer it to a serving platter. Garnish with chopped fresh dill or parsley and serve with lemon wedges on the side.
8. Enjoy: Serve the grilled salmon hot and enjoy its delicious flavor and tender texture!

Grilled salmon pairs well with a variety of side dishes, such as grilled vegetables, rice, quinoa, or a fresh salad. It's perfect for a summertime barbecue or a quick and healthy weeknight dinner.

Zucchini Noodles with Marinara

Ingredients:

- 4 medium zucchinis
- 2 tablespoons olive oil
- 2 cloves garlic, minced
- 1 can (14 ounces) crushed tomatoes
- 1 teaspoon dried oregano
- 1 teaspoon dried basil
- 1/2 teaspoon onion powder
- Salt and pepper, to taste
- Grated Parmesan cheese, for serving (optional)
- Fresh basil leaves, chopped, for garnish (optional)

Instructions:

1. Prepare Zucchini Noodles: Using a spiralizer or a julienne peeler, spiralize the zucchinis into noodles. If you prefer softer noodles, you can blanch them in boiling water for 1-2 minutes, then drain and set aside. Otherwise, you can use them raw for a crunchy texture.
2. Make Marinara Sauce: In a large skillet, heat the olive oil over medium heat. Add the minced garlic and sauté for 1 minute until fragrant.
3. Add Tomatoes and Spices: Pour the crushed tomatoes into the skillet with the garlic. Stir in the dried oregano, dried basil, onion powder, salt, and pepper. Bring the sauce to a simmer and let it cook for 5-10 minutes, stirring occasionally, to allow the flavors to meld together and the sauce to thicken slightly.
4. Cook Zucchini Noodles: If you haven't already blanched the zucchini noodles, add them directly to the skillet with the marinara sauce. Cook for 2-3 minutes, tossing gently with tongs, until the noodles are heated through and coated evenly with the sauce. Be careful not to overcook the noodles, as they can become mushy.
5. Serve: Transfer the zucchini noodles with marinara sauce to serving plates or bowls. If desired, sprinkle grated Parmesan cheese on top and garnish with chopped fresh basil leaves.
6. Enjoy: Serve the zucchini noodles with marinara sauce hot and enjoy a delicious and nutritious low-carb meal!

This zucchini noodles with marinara sauce recipe is light, flavorful, and perfect for a quick and healthy weeknight dinner. You can also customize it by adding your favorite toppings such as cooked mushrooms, olives, or grilled chicken.

Chicken and Vegetable Stir-Fry

Ingredients:

- 2 boneless, skinless chicken breasts, thinly sliced
- 2 tablespoons soy sauce
- 1 tablespoon oyster sauce (optional)
- 2 cloves garlic, minced
- 1 teaspoon ginger, minced
- 2 tablespoons vegetable oil, divided
- 1 bell pepper, thinly sliced
- 1 carrot, julienned or thinly sliced
- 1 cup broccoli florets
- 1 cup snap peas or snow peas
- 1 cup sliced mushrooms
- Salt and pepper, to taste
- Cooked rice or noodles, for serving
- Optional garnish: chopped green onions, sesame seeds

Instructions:

1. Marinate Chicken: In a bowl, combine the thinly sliced chicken breasts with 1 tablespoon of soy sauce and the optional oyster sauce. Let it marinate for at least 15 minutes, or while you prepare the vegetables.
2. Prepare Sauce: In a small bowl, mix the remaining tablespoon of soy sauce with minced garlic and ginger. Set aside.
3. Heat Oil: Heat 1 tablespoon of vegetable oil in a large skillet or wok over medium-high heat.
4. Cook Chicken: Add the marinated chicken to the skillet in a single layer. Cook for 3-4 minutes, stirring occasionally, until the chicken is cooked through and no longer pink. Remove the chicken from the skillet and set aside.
5. Cook Vegetables: In the same skillet, add the remaining tablespoon of vegetable oil. Add the sliced bell pepper, julienned carrot, broccoli florets, snap peas, and sliced mushrooms. Stir-fry for 4-5 minutes, or until the vegetables are tender-crisp.
6. Combine: Return the cooked chicken to the skillet with the vegetables. Pour the sauce over the chicken and vegetables. Stir well to combine and coat everything evenly. Cook for an additional 1-2 minutes to heat through.
7. Season: Taste and adjust the seasoning with salt and pepper, if needed.

8. Serve: Serve the chicken and vegetable stir-fry hot over cooked rice or noodles. Garnish with chopped green onions and sesame seeds, if desired.
9. Enjoy: Enjoy your delicious homemade chicken and vegetable stir-fry!

This chicken and vegetable stir-fry is versatile, so feel free to use any combination of vegetables you prefer or have on hand. It's a great way to get a nutritious meal on the table in no time!

Baked Chicken Tenders

Ingredients:

- 1 lb chicken breast tenders
- 1 cup breadcrumbs (plain or seasoned)
- 1/4 cup grated Parmesan cheese
- 1 teaspoon garlic powder
- 1 teaspoon paprika
- 1/2 teaspoon salt
- 1/4 teaspoon black pepper
- 2 eggs, beaten
- Cooking spray or olive oil

Instructions:

1. Preheat Oven: Preheat your oven to 400°F (200°C). Line a baking sheet with parchment paper or aluminum foil and lightly coat it with cooking spray or olive oil.
2. Prepare Breading: In a shallow dish, combine the breadcrumbs, grated Parmesan cheese, garlic powder, paprika, salt, and black pepper. Mix well to combine.
3. Coat Chicken: Dip each chicken tender into the beaten eggs, then coat it with the breadcrumb mixture, pressing gently to adhere. Place the coated chicken tenders on the prepared baking sheet.
4. Bake: Once all the chicken tenders are coated and arranged on the baking sheet, lightly spray the tops of the chicken tenders with cooking spray or drizzle with olive oil. This will help them brown and crisp up in the oven. Bake in the preheated oven for 15-20 minutes, or until the chicken tenders are cooked through and golden brown, flipping halfway through the baking time for even browning.
5. Serve: Once baked, remove the chicken tenders from the oven and let them cool for a few minutes before serving.
6. Enjoy: Serve the baked chicken tenders hot with your favorite dipping sauce, such as barbecue sauce, honey mustard, or ranch dressing.

These baked chicken tenders are crispy on the outside, tender and juicy on the inside, and full of flavor. They make a great appetizer, snack, or main course for both kids and adults. Plus, they're healthier than their fried counterparts, making them a guilt-free option for any meal!

Lentil Sloppy Joes

Ingredients:

- 1 cup dry lentils (green or brown), rinsed and drained
- 3 cups vegetable broth or water
- 1 tablespoon olive oil
- 1 onion, finely chopped
- 2 cloves garlic, minced
- 1 bell pepper, diced
- 1 carrot, grated
- 1 can (14 ounces) crushed tomatoes
- 2 tablespoons tomato paste
- 2 tablespoons soy sauce or tamari
- 1 tablespoon Worcestershire sauce (optional)
- 1 tablespoon maple syrup or brown sugar
- 1 teaspoon chili powder
- 1/2 teaspoon smoked paprika
- Salt and pepper, to taste
- Hamburger buns, for serving

Instructions:

1. Cook Lentils: In a medium saucepan, combine the dry lentils and vegetable broth or water. Bring to a boil, then reduce the heat to low, cover, and simmer for 20-25 minutes, or until the lentils are tender and most of the liquid is absorbed. Drain any excess liquid and set aside.
2. Sauté Vegetables: In a large skillet or saucepan, heat the olive oil over medium heat. Add the chopped onion, minced garlic, diced bell pepper, and grated carrot. Cook for 5-6 minutes, or until the vegetables are softened.
3. Add Remaining Ingredients: Stir in the cooked lentils, crushed tomatoes, tomato paste, soy sauce or tamari, Worcestershire sauce (if using), maple syrup or brown sugar, chili powder, smoked paprika, salt, and pepper. Mix well to combine.
4. Simmer: Reduce the heat to low and let the lentil mixture simmer for 10-15 minutes, stirring occasionally, to allow the flavors to meld together and the mixture to thicken slightly.
5. Adjust Seasoning: Taste the lentil sloppy joe mixture and adjust the seasoning as needed, adding more salt, pepper, or spices to taste.
6. Serve: To serve, spoon the lentil sloppy joe mixture onto hamburger buns. You can toast the buns if desired. Serve hot and enjoy!

These lentil sloppy joes are hearty, flavorful, and perfect for a meatless meal option that the whole family will love. Serve them with your favorite side dishes, such as coleslaw, potato salad, or oven-baked fries, for a delicious and satisfying meal.

Baked Fish Tacos

Ingredients:

- 1 lb white fish fillets (such as cod, tilapia, or mahi-mahi)
- 2 tablespoons olive oil
- 1 teaspoon chili powder
- 1/2 teaspoon ground cumin
- 1/2 teaspoon paprika
- 1/4 teaspoon garlic powder
- 1/4 teaspoon onion powder
- Salt and pepper, to taste
- 8 small corn or flour tortillas
- Cabbage slaw (see recipe below)
- Sliced avocado
- Fresh cilantro, chopped
- Lime wedges, for serving

Cabbage Slaw Ingredients:

- 2 cups shredded cabbage or coleslaw mix
- 2 tablespoons Greek yogurt or sour cream
- 1 tablespoon mayonnaise
- 1 tablespoon lime juice
- 1 teaspoon honey or maple syrup
- Salt and pepper, to taste

Instructions:

1. Preheat Oven: Preheat your oven to 400°F (200°C). Line a baking sheet with parchment paper or aluminum foil.
2. Prepare Fish: Pat the fish fillets dry with paper towels. In a small bowl, mix together the olive oil, chili powder, cumin, paprika, garlic powder, onion powder, salt, and pepper. Rub the spice mixture evenly over both sides of the fish fillets.
3. Bake: Place the seasoned fish fillets on the prepared baking sheet. Bake in the preheated oven for 12-15 minutes, or until the fish is cooked through and flakes easily with a fork.
4. Prepare Cabbage Slaw: While the fish is baking, prepare the cabbage slaw. In a medium bowl, whisk together the Greek yogurt (or sour cream), mayonnaise, lime juice, honey (or maple syrup), salt, and pepper. Add the shredded cabbage or coleslaw mix to the bowl and toss until evenly coated with the dressing.

5. Warm Tortillas: In the last few minutes of baking the fish, wrap the tortillas in aluminum foil and place them in the oven to warm through.
6. Assemble Tacos: Once the fish is cooked, remove it from the oven and use a fork to flake it into bite-sized pieces. To assemble the tacos, place some flaked fish onto each warmed tortilla. Top with cabbage slaw, sliced avocado, and chopped cilantro. Squeeze a lime wedge over each taco before serving.
7. Serve: Serve the baked fish tacos immediately, with extra lime wedges on the side for squeezing.

These baked fish tacos are fresh, flavorful, and perfect for a light and healthy meal. Enjoy the combination of tender baked fish, crunchy cabbage slaw, creamy avocado, and tangy lime!

Sweet Potato and Black Bean Enchiladas

Ingredients:

- 2 medium sweet potatoes, peeled and diced
- 1 can (15 ounces) black beans, drained and rinsed
- 1 cup corn kernels (fresh, canned, or frozen)
- 1 bell pepper, diced
- 1 small onion, diced
- 2 cloves garlic, minced
- 1 teaspoon ground cumin
- 1 teaspoon chili powder
- 1/2 teaspoon smoked paprika
- Salt and pepper, to taste
- 1 cup enchilada sauce (store-bought or homemade)
- 8 small corn or flour tortillas
- 1 cup shredded cheese (cheddar, Monterey Jack, or Mexican blend)
- Fresh cilantro, chopped, for garnish
- Optional toppings: diced avocado, sour cream, salsa, lime wedges

Instructions:

1. Preheat Oven: Preheat your oven to 375°F (190°C). Lightly grease a 9x13-inch baking dish with cooking spray or olive oil.
2. Cook Sweet Potatoes: Place the diced sweet potatoes in a microwave-safe bowl and cover with water. Microwave on high for 5-6 minutes, or until the sweet potatoes are tender. Drain and set aside.
3. Prepare Filling: In a large skillet, heat olive oil over medium heat. Add the diced onion and bell pepper, and cook for 5-6 minutes until softened. Add the minced garlic, ground cumin, chili powder, smoked paprika, salt, and pepper. Cook for an additional 1-2 minutes until fragrant. Stir in the cooked sweet potatoes, black beans, and corn kernels. Cook for another 2-3 minutes until heated through. Remove from heat.
4. Assemble Enchiladas: Spread a thin layer of enchilada sauce on the bottom of the prepared baking dish. Spoon the sweet potato and black bean mixture onto each tortilla and roll it up tightly. Place the filled tortillas seam-side down in the baking dish, arranging them side by side.
5. Top with Sauce and Cheese: Pour the remaining enchilada sauce evenly over the top of the filled tortillas. Sprinkle shredded cheese on top.

6. Bake: Cover the baking dish with aluminum foil and bake in the preheated oven for 20-25 minutes, or until the enchiladas are heated through and the cheese is melted and bubbly.
7. Serve: Remove the foil from the baking dish and garnish the enchiladas with chopped cilantro. Serve hot with optional toppings such as diced avocado, sour cream, salsa, and lime wedges.

These sweet potato and black bean enchiladas are flavorful, hearty, and packed with nutritious ingredients. They're sure to be a hit with your family and friends! Enjoy them for a delicious and satisfying meal.

Veggie Pizza on Whole Wheat Crust

Ingredients:

- 1 whole wheat pizza crust (store-bought or homemade)
- 1/2 cup tomato sauce or pizza sauce
- 1 cup shredded mozzarella cheese (part-skim or vegan cheese)
- Assorted vegetables, thinly sliced or diced (such as bell peppers, onions, mushrooms, cherry tomatoes, spinach, broccoli, olives, etc.)
- Olive oil, for drizzling
- Salt and pepper, to taste
- Optional toppings: fresh basil, crushed red pepper flakes, grated Parmesan cheese (for non-vegan version)

Instructions:

1. Preheat Oven: Preheat your oven to the temperature specified on the pizza crust package or recipe instructions.
2. Prepare Crust: Place the whole wheat pizza crust on a baking sheet or pizza stone.
3. Assemble Pizza: Spread the tomato sauce or pizza sauce evenly over the surface of the pizza crust, leaving a small border around the edges for the crust. Sprinkle the shredded mozzarella cheese evenly over the sauce.
4. Add Vegetables: Arrange the assorted vegetables on top of the cheese, distributing them evenly across the pizza. Feel free to get creative with your veggie combinations!
5. Season: Drizzle a little olive oil over the vegetables and sprinkle with salt and pepper to taste.
6. Bake: Place the pizza in the preheated oven and bake according to the crust package or recipe instructions, usually for about 12-15 minutes, or until the crust is golden brown and the cheese is melted and bubbly.
7. Serve: Remove the veggie pizza from the oven and let it cool for a few minutes before slicing. Garnish with fresh basil, crushed red pepper flakes, and grated Parmesan cheese, if desired.
8. Enjoy: Slice the whole wheat veggie pizza and serve hot as a delicious and nutritious meal!

This whole wheat veggie pizza is a great way to incorporate more vegetables into your diet while still enjoying a classic favorite. It's perfect for a quick and easy weeknight dinner or as a crowd-pleasing option for parties and gatherings. Feel free to customize the toppings to suit your taste preferences!

Grilled Portobello Mushrooms

Ingredients:

- 4 large portobello mushrooms
- 2 tablespoons balsamic vinegar
- 2 tablespoons olive oil
- 2 cloves garlic, minced
- 1 teaspoon dried thyme
- Salt and pepper, to taste
- Optional toppings: fresh herbs (such as parsley or basil), grated Parmesan cheese, crumbled feta cheese, balsamic glaze

Instructions:

1. Prepare Mushrooms: Clean the portobello mushrooms by wiping them with a damp paper towel to remove any dirt. Remove the stems by gently twisting them off or using a knife. Use a spoon to scrape out the gills from the underside of the mushrooms, if desired (this step is optional but can help prevent the mushrooms from becoming too watery during grilling).
2. Marinate: In a shallow dish, whisk together the balsamic vinegar, olive oil, minced garlic, dried thyme, salt, and pepper. Place the cleaned portobello mushrooms in the marinade, turning them to coat evenly. Let them marinate for at least 15-30 minutes, flipping them once halfway through.
3. Preheat Grill: Preheat your grill to medium-high heat. If using a charcoal grill, wait until the coals are hot and covered with ash.
4. Grill: Once the grill is hot, place the marinated portobello mushrooms on the grill grates, gill-side down. Grill for 4-5 minutes, then flip them over and continue grilling for another 4-5 minutes, or until the mushrooms are tender and lightly charred.
5. Serve: Remove the grilled portobello mushrooms from the grill and transfer them to a serving platter. If desired, sprinkle with fresh herbs, grated Parmesan cheese, crumbled feta cheese, or drizzle with balsamic glaze before serving.
6. Enjoy: Serve the grilled portobello mushrooms hot as a delicious and flavorful dish. They're perfect as a standalone meal, served alongside grilled vegetables and grains, or used as a meaty topping for salads, pasta, or sandwiches.

These grilled portobello mushrooms are savory, juicy, and packed with flavor. They make a great option for vegetarians and meat-lovers alike, and they're sure to be a hit at your next barbecue or cookout!

Whole Wheat Pancakes

Ingredients:

- 1 cup whole wheat flour
- 1 tablespoon sugar or sweetener of choice (optional)
- 1 teaspoon baking powder
- 1/2 teaspoon baking soda
- 1/4 teaspoon salt
- 1 cup milk (dairy or plant-based)
- 1 large egg
- 2 tablespoons melted butter or oil
- 1 teaspoon vanilla extract (optional)
- Additional butter or oil for cooking
- Maple syrup, fresh fruit, or toppings of choice for serving

Instructions:

1. Preheat Griddle or Pan: Preheat a griddle or non-stick skillet over medium heat. Lightly grease the surface with butter or oil.
2. Mix Dry Ingredients: In a large mixing bowl, whisk together the whole wheat flour, sugar (if using), baking powder, baking soda, and salt.
3. Combine Wet Ingredients: In a separate bowl, whisk together the milk, egg, melted butter or oil, and vanilla extract (if using).
4. Combine Mixtures: Pour the wet ingredients into the dry ingredients and stir until just combined. Be careful not to overmix; a few lumps are okay. If the batter is too thick, you can add a little more milk until you reach your desired consistency.
5. Cook Pancakes: Pour about 1/4 cup of batter onto the preheated griddle or skillet for each pancake. Cook until bubbles form on the surface of the pancake and the edges begin to look set, about 2-3 minutes.
6. Flip: Carefully flip the pancakes with a spatula and cook for an additional 1-2 minutes on the other side, until golden brown and cooked through.
7. Serve: Transfer the cooked pancakes to a serving plate and keep warm while you cook the remaining batter. Serve the whole wheat pancakes hot with maple syrup, fresh fruit, or your favorite toppings.
8. Enjoy: Enjoy your wholesome and delicious whole wheat pancakes as a nutritious breakfast or brunch option!

These whole wheat pancakes are not only tasty but also packed with fiber and nutrients from the whole wheat flour. They're sure to become a favorite in your breakfast rotation!

Feel free to customize them with additional ingredients such as nuts, seeds, or spices to suit your taste preferences.

Greek Yogurt Parfaits

Ingredients:

- 2 cups Greek yogurt (plain or flavored)
- 1 cup granola
- 1 cup mixed berries (such as strawberries, blueberries, raspberries)
- Honey or maple syrup, for drizzling (optional)
- Nuts or seeds (such as almonds, walnuts, chia seeds) for topping (optional)
- Fresh mint leaves, for garnish (optional)

Instructions:

1. **Prepare Ingredients:** Wash the berries and pat them dry with paper towels. If using large berries like strawberries, slice them into smaller pieces.
2. **Layer Parfaits:** Begin by spooning a layer of Greek yogurt into the bottom of serving glasses or bowls. Use about 1/4 cup of Greek yogurt for each parfait.
3. **Add Granola:** Sprinkle a layer of granola over the Greek yogurt in each glass. Use about 2-3 tablespoons of granola for each parfait.
4. **Add Berries:** Top the granola layer with a generous spoonful of mixed berries. Use a variety of berries to add color and flavor to your parfaits.
5. **Repeat Layers:** Repeat the layering process with another layer of Greek yogurt, granola, and berries until you reach the top of the serving glasses or bowls. Finish with a final dollop of Greek yogurt on top.
6. **Drizzle with Honey:** If desired, drizzle a little honey or maple syrup over the top of each parfait for added sweetness.
7. **Top with Nuts or Seeds:** Sprinkle with nuts or seeds for extra crunch and protein, if desired.
8. **Garnish:** Garnish each parfait with a fresh mint leaf for a pop of color and freshness, if desired.
9. **Serve:** Serve the Greek yogurt parfaits immediately, or cover and refrigerate until ready to serve. Enjoy them as a nutritious breakfast, snack, or dessert!

These Greek yogurt parfaits are not only delicious but also packed with protein, fiber, vitamins, and minerals. They're customizable based on your preferences and make a great option for a quick and healthy meal or snack on the go. Feel free to experiment with different flavors of Greek yogurt, granola, and toppings to create your perfect parfait!

Baked Apple Chips

Ingredients:

- 2 large apples (any variety you prefer)
- 1 tablespoon lemon juice (optional, to prevent browning)
- 1 teaspoon ground cinnamon (optional, for flavor)

Instructions:

1. Preheat Oven: Preheat your oven to 200°F (95°C). Line a baking sheet with parchment paper or a silicone baking mat.
2. Prepare Apples: Wash the apples thoroughly under running water. Core the apples and slice them thinly into rounds, about 1/8 inch thick. You can use a mandoline slicer for uniform slices, or carefully slice them by hand.
3. Optional Lemon Juice: If desired, you can toss the apple slices with lemon juice in a bowl. This helps prevent browning and adds a tangy flavor to the chips. However, if you prefer the natural sweetness of the apples, you can skip this step.
4. Arrange Slices: Place the apple slices in a single layer on the prepared baking sheet. Make sure the slices are not overlapping to ensure even baking.
5. Optional Cinnamon: If desired, sprinkle ground cinnamon evenly over the apple slices for added flavor. You can also experiment with other spices such as nutmeg or pumpkin pie spice.
6. Bake: Transfer the baking sheet to the preheated oven and bake the apple slices for 1.5 to 2 hours, or until they are dried out and crispy. The exact baking time will depend on the thickness of your apple slices and the moisture content of the apples.
7. Cool: Once the apple chips are done baking, remove them from the oven and let them cool completely on the baking sheet. As they cool, they will continue to crisp up.
8. Serve: Once cooled, transfer the baked apple chips to an airtight container or zip-top bag for storage. Enjoy them as a healthy snack on their own, or serve them with yogurt, nut butter, or cheese for a delicious and satisfying treat.

These baked apple chips are crispy, sweet, and full of natural apple flavor. They're a great alternative to store-bought chips and are perfect for satisfying your crunchy cravings in a healthier way. Plus, they're easy to make and can be customized with your favorite spices and seasonings!

Turkey and Avocado Wraps

Ingredients:

- 4 large whole wheat or spinach tortillas
- 8 slices deli turkey breast
- 1 large ripe avocado, thinly sliced
- 1 cup shredded lettuce or spinach leaves
- 1 medium tomato, thinly sliced
- 1/2 cup thinly sliced red onion (optional)
- 1/4 cup mayonnaise or Greek yogurt
- 2 tablespoons Dijon mustard (optional)
- Salt and pepper, to taste

Instructions:

1. Prepare Ingredients: Lay out the tortillas on a clean work surface. Arrange the turkey slices evenly over the tortillas, leaving a border around the edges for rolling.
2. Add Avocado: Place the thinly sliced avocado over the turkey slices, followed by the shredded lettuce or spinach leaves.
3. Add Tomato and Onion: Place the tomato slices and thinly sliced red onion (if using) evenly over the avocado and lettuce.
4. Season: Season the toppings with salt and pepper to taste.
5. Spread Sauce: In a small bowl, mix together the mayonnaise or Greek yogurt with the Dijon mustard (if using). Spread the sauce evenly over the toppings on each tortilla.
6. Roll: Starting from one edge, tightly roll up each tortilla into a wrap, tucking in the sides as you go to keep the filling secure.
7. Slice and Serve: Use a sharp knife to slice each wrap in half diagonally, creating two halves. Serve immediately, or wrap each half tightly in plastic wrap or parchment paper for easy transport.
8. Enjoy: Enjoy your turkey and avocado wraps as a delicious and nutritious meal on the go or at home!

These turkey and avocado wraps are packed with protein, healthy fats, and plenty of fresh veggies, making them a satisfying and wholesome meal option. Feel free to customize the wraps with your favorite ingredients, such as adding sliced cheese, bacon, or roasted vegetables for extra flavor and variety.

Veggie Omelette

Ingredients:

- 3 eggs
- 1/4 cup chopped bell peppers (any color you like)
- 1/4 cup chopped onion
- 1/4 cup chopped mushrooms
- 1/4 cup chopped tomatoes
- Salt and pepper to taste
- 1 tablespoon olive oil
- Optional: grated cheese (cheddar, mozzarella, or your favorite)

Instructions:

1. Heat the olive oil in a non-stick skillet over medium heat.
2. Add the chopped bell peppers, onions, and mushrooms to the skillet. Sauté them for about 3-4 minutes until they are tender.
3. In a bowl, beat the eggs with a pinch of salt and pepper.
4. Pour the beaten eggs into the skillet over the sautéed veggies.
5. Let the eggs cook for about 2 minutes until the edges start to set.
6. Using a spatula, gently lift the edges of the omelette and tilt the skillet to let the uncooked eggs flow to the bottom.
7. Once the eggs are mostly set but still slightly runny on top, add the chopped tomatoes (and grated cheese if using) over one half of the omelette.
8. Carefully fold the other half of the omelette over the filling using the spatula.
9. Cook for another 1-2 minutes until the eggs are fully set and the cheese is melted (if using).
10. Slide the omelette onto a plate and serve hot.

You can customize this recipe by adding your favorite veggies like spinach, zucchini, or broccoli, and even some herbs like parsley or basil for extra flavor. Enjoy your veggie omelette!

Stuffed Acorn Squash

Ingredients:

- 2 acorn squash
- 1 tablespoon olive oil
- 1 small onion, diced
- 2 cloves garlic, minced
- 1 cup quinoa, rinsed
- 2 cups vegetable broth or water
- 1 teaspoon dried thyme
- 1 teaspoon dried sage
- Salt and pepper to taste
- 1/2 cup dried cranberries or raisins
- 1/2 cup chopped pecans or walnuts
- Optional: grated Parmesan cheese or crumbled feta cheese

Instructions:

1. Preheat your oven to 400°F (200°C).
2. Cut the acorn squash in half lengthwise and scoop out the seeds and stringy pulp with a spoon.
3. Place the squash halves, cut side up, on a baking sheet lined with parchment paper or aluminum foil. Brush the flesh with olive oil and sprinkle with salt and pepper.
4. Roast the squash in the preheated oven for about 30-40 minutes, or until the flesh is tender when pierced with a fork.
5. While the squash is roasting, prepare the filling. In a large skillet, heat the olive oil over medium heat. Add the diced onion and minced garlic and sauté until softened, about 3-4 minutes.
6. Add the quinoa to the skillet and toast it for 1-2 minutes, stirring constantly.
7. Pour in the vegetable broth or water and add the dried thyme, dried sage, salt, and pepper. Bring the mixture to a boil, then reduce the heat to low, cover, and simmer for 15-20 minutes, or until the quinoa is cooked and the liquid is absorbed.
8. Remove the skillet from the heat and stir in the dried cranberries or raisins and chopped pecans or walnuts.
9. Once the squash is done roasting, remove it from the oven and let it cool slightly.
10. Fill each squash half with the quinoa stuffing mixture, pressing it down gently.

11. If desired, sprinkle grated Parmesan cheese or crumbled feta cheese over the top of each stuffed squash half.
12. Return the stuffed squash to the oven and bake for an additional 10-15 minutes, or until the filling is heated through and the cheese is melted and bubbly.
13. Serve the stuffed acorn squash hot, garnished with fresh herbs if desired. Enjoy!

This dish makes for a beautiful and satisfying main course or side dish, perfect for a cozy autumn or winter meal. Feel free to customize the filling with your favorite ingredients, such as diced apples, spinach, or cooked chickpeas.

Spinach and Feta Stuffed Chicken Breast

Ingredients:

- 2 large boneless, skinless chicken breasts
- Salt and pepper to taste
- 1 tablespoon olive oil
- 2 cups fresh spinach, chopped
- 2 cloves garlic, minced
- 1/2 cup crumbled feta cheese
- 1/4 cup grated Parmesan cheese
- 1/4 teaspoon dried oregano
- 1/4 teaspoon dried basil
- Toothpicks or kitchen twine

Instructions:

1. Preheat your oven to 375°F (190°C).
2. Season the chicken breasts with salt and pepper on both sides.
3. In a skillet, heat the olive oil over medium heat. Add the minced garlic and cook for about 1 minute until fragrant.
4. Add the chopped spinach to the skillet and sauté until wilted, about 2-3 minutes.
5. Remove the skillet from the heat and stir in the crumbled feta cheese, grated Parmesan cheese, dried oregano, and dried basil. Mix until well combined.
6. Use a sharp knife to make a horizontal slit along the side of each chicken breast, creating a pocket for the stuffing. Be careful not to cut all the way through.
7. Stuff each chicken breast with the spinach and feta mixture, dividing it evenly between the two breasts. Secure the openings with toothpicks or tie with kitchen twine to keep the filling inside.
8. Place the stuffed chicken breasts in a baking dish or on a baking sheet lined with parchment paper.
9. Bake in the preheated oven for 25-30 minutes, or until the chicken is cooked through and no longer pink in the center, and the juices run clear. The internal temperature of the chicken should reach 165°F (74°C).
10. Once cooked, remove the toothpicks or twine from the chicken breasts.
11. Allow the stuffed chicken breasts to rest for a few minutes before serving to allow the juices to redistribute.
12. Serve the spinach and feta stuffed chicken breasts hot, garnished with fresh herbs if desired. Enjoy!

This dish pairs well with a side of roasted vegetables, mashed potatoes, or a simple salad for a complete and satisfying meal.

Cauliflower Pizza Crust

Ingredients:

- 1 medium head of cauliflower, washed and dried
- 1/4 cup grated Parmesan cheese
- 1/4 cup shredded mozzarella cheese
- 1/2 teaspoon dried oregano
- 1/2 teaspoon dried basil
- 1/2 teaspoon garlic powder
- 1/4 teaspoon salt
- 1/4 teaspoon black pepper
- 1 large egg, beaten
- Optional toppings: pizza sauce, shredded cheese, vegetables, meats, etc.

Instructions:

1. Preheat your oven to 400°F (200°C). Line a baking sheet with parchment paper or lightly grease it with olive oil.
2. Cut the cauliflower into florets and discard the core. Place the florets in a food processor and pulse until they resemble fine crumbs, similar to rice.
3. Transfer the cauliflower crumbs to a microwave-safe bowl and microwave on high for 4-5 minutes, or until softened. Alternatively, you can steam the cauliflower on the stovetop until tender.
4. Once the cauliflower is cooked, let it cool for a few minutes, then transfer it to a clean kitchen towel or cheesecloth. Squeeze out as much moisture as possible from the cauliflower. This step is crucial to prevent a soggy crust.
5. In a mixing bowl, combine the squeezed cauliflower with the grated Parmesan cheese, shredded mozzarella cheese, dried oregano, dried basil, garlic powder, salt, and black pepper. Mix until well combined.
6. Add the beaten egg to the cauliflower mixture and mix until a dough forms.
7. Place the cauliflower dough onto the prepared baking sheet and use your hands to shape it into a thin, round crust, about 1/4 inch thick. Make sure to press it evenly to avoid any thin spots.
8. Bake the cauliflower crust in the preheated oven for 20-25 minutes, or until golden brown and firm to the touch.
9. Once the crust is baked, remove it from the oven and add your desired toppings, such as pizza sauce, shredded cheese, vegetables, and meats.
10. Return the pizza to the oven and bake for an additional 10-15 minutes, or until the cheese is melted and bubbly.

11. Once cooked, remove the cauliflower pizza from the oven and let it cool for a few minutes before slicing and serving.
12. Enjoy your homemade cauliflower pizza crust with your favorite toppings!

This cauliflower pizza crust is gluten-free and packed with flavor, making it a healthier option for pizza night. Feel free to get creative with your toppings and customize it to your taste preferences.

Kale and Quinoa Salad

Ingredients:

For the salad:

- 1 cup quinoa, rinsed
- 2 cups water or vegetable broth
- 1 bunch kale, stems removed and leaves chopped
- 1 tablespoon olive oil
- 1/4 teaspoon salt
- 1/4 teaspoon black pepper
- 1/2 cup cherry tomatoes, halved
- 1/2 cup cucumber, diced
- 1/4 cup red onion, thinly sliced
- 1/4 cup toasted pine nuts or almonds
- Optional: crumbled feta cheese or grated Parmesan cheese

For the dressing:

- 3 tablespoons extra virgin olive oil
- 2 tablespoons lemon juice (about 1 lemon)
- 1 clove garlic, minced
- 1 teaspoon Dijon mustard
- 1 teaspoon honey or maple syrup
- Salt and pepper to taste

Instructions:

1. In a medium saucepan, combine the quinoa and water or vegetable broth. Bring to a boil over high heat, then reduce the heat to low, cover, and simmer for 15-20 minutes, or until the quinoa is cooked and the liquid is absorbed. Remove from heat and let it cool slightly.
2. While the quinoa is cooking, prepare the kale. Place the chopped kale in a large bowl and drizzle with 1 tablespoon of olive oil. Massage the kale leaves with your hands for a few minutes until they soften and become brighter in color. Sprinkle with salt and pepper to taste.
3. In a small bowl, whisk together the extra virgin olive oil, lemon juice, minced garlic, Dijon mustard, honey or maple syrup, salt, and pepper to make the dressing.

4. Once the quinoa is cooked and slightly cooled, add it to the bowl with the massaged kale. Add the cherry tomatoes, diced cucumber, sliced red onion, and toasted pine nuts or almonds.
5. Pour the dressing over the salad and toss everything together until well combined.
6. If desired, sprinkle crumbled feta cheese or grated Parmesan cheese over the top of the salad.
7. Serve the kale and quinoa salad immediately, or refrigerate it for a few hours to allow the flavors to meld together.
8. Enjoy your nutritious and delicious kale and quinoa salad as a light lunch or side dish!

This salad is versatile, so feel free to customize it with your favorite ingredients or add protein such as grilled chicken or chickpeas for a heartier meal.

Broccoli Cheddar Soup (lightened)

Ingredients:

- 2 tablespoons olive oil or unsalted butter
- 1 onion, chopped
- 2 cloves garlic, minced
- 3 cups broccoli florets
- 2 medium carrots, peeled and diced
- 3 cups low-sodium vegetable broth
- 1 cup low-fat milk or unsweetened almond milk
- 1/4 cup all-purpose flour
- 1 cup shredded sharp cheddar cheese
- Salt and pepper to taste
- Optional garnish: additional shredded cheddar cheese, chopped green onions, or croutons

Instructions:

1. In a large pot or Dutch oven, heat the olive oil or butter over medium heat. Add the chopped onion and garlic and sauté for 2-3 minutes until softened and fragrant.
2. Add the broccoli florets and diced carrots to the pot. Cook for another 5 minutes, stirring occasionally, until the vegetables start to soften.
3. Sprinkle the flour over the vegetables and stir to coat evenly. Cook for 1-2 minutes to cook out the raw flour taste.
4. Gradually pour in the vegetable broth, stirring constantly to prevent lumps from forming. Bring the mixture to a simmer and cook for 10-15 minutes, or until the vegetables are tender.
5. Using an immersion blender or transferring the soup to a blender in batches, blend the soup until smooth and creamy.
6. Return the soup to the pot if necessary and stir in the low-fat milk or almond milk. Heat the soup over medium heat until warmed through.
7. Stir in the shredded cheddar cheese until melted and smooth. Season with salt and pepper to taste.
8. Ladle the soup into bowls and garnish with additional shredded cheddar cheese, chopped green onions, or croutons if desired.
9. Serve the lightened broccoli cheddar soup hot and enjoy!

This lighter version of broccoli cheddar soup is still creamy and flavorful, but with less fat and calories compared to traditional recipes. It's a comforting and satisfying dish that's perfect for a cozy meal any day of the week.

Shrimp and Veggie Skewers

Ingredients:

- 1 pound large shrimp, peeled and deveined
- 2 bell peppers (any color), cut into chunks
- 1 red onion, cut into chunks
- 1 zucchini, sliced
- 1 yellow squash, sliced
- Cherry tomatoes
- Wooden or metal skewers (if using wooden skewers, soak them in water for 30 minutes to prevent burning)

For the marinade:

- 1/4 cup olive oil
- 2 cloves garlic, minced
- 2 tablespoons lemon juice
- 1 teaspoon dried oregano
- 1 teaspoon dried basil
- Salt and pepper to taste

Instructions:

1. In a bowl, whisk together the olive oil, minced garlic, lemon juice, dried oregano, dried basil, salt, and pepper to make the marinade.
2. Place the shrimp in a separate bowl and pour half of the marinade over them. Toss to coat the shrimp evenly, then cover and refrigerate for at least 30 minutes to marinate.
3. Meanwhile, prepare the vegetables. Cut the bell peppers, red onion, zucchini, and yellow squash into chunks or slices, depending on your preference.
4. Thread the marinated shrimp, bell peppers, red onion, zucchini, yellow squash, and cherry tomatoes onto the skewers, alternating between ingredients.
5. Preheat your grill to medium-high heat or preheat your oven to 400°F (200°C).
6. If using a grill, lightly oil the grates to prevent sticking. Place the skewers on the grill and cook for 2-3 minutes per side, or until the shrimp are pink and opaque and the vegetables are tender and slightly charred.
7. If using an oven, place the skewers on a baking sheet lined with parchment paper or aluminum foil. Roast in the preheated oven for 10-12 minutes, or until the shrimp are pink and opaque and the vegetables are tender.

8. Remove the shrimp and veggie skewers from the grill or oven and transfer them to a serving platter.
9. Drizzle the remaining marinade over the skewers for extra flavor, if desired.
10. Serve the shrimp and veggie skewers hot, garnished with chopped fresh herbs like parsley or basil, if desired.

These shrimp and veggie skewers are perfect for a summer barbecue or a simple weeknight dinner. They're light, flavorful, and packed with protein and nutrients from the shrimp and vegetables. Enjoy!

Brown Rice Risotto

Ingredients:

- 1 cup brown rice
- 4 cups low-sodium vegetable or chicken broth
- 2 tablespoons olive oil or butter
- 1 onion, finely chopped
- 2 cloves garlic, minced
- 1 cup mushrooms, sliced
- 1/2 cup dry white wine (optional)
- 1/2 cup grated Parmesan cheese
- Salt and pepper to taste
- Fresh herbs for garnish (such as parsley or thyme)

Instructions:

1. In a medium saucepan, bring the vegetable or chicken broth to a simmer over medium heat. Keep it warm while you prepare the risotto.
2. In a separate large skillet or saucepan, heat the olive oil or butter over medium heat. Add the chopped onion and sauté for 2-3 minutes until softened.
3. Add the minced garlic to the skillet and cook for another minute until fragrant.
4. Add the sliced mushrooms to the skillet and cook for 5-7 minutes until they release their moisture and start to brown.
5. Stir in the brown rice and cook for 1-2 minutes, stirring constantly, until the rice is lightly toasted.
6. If using, pour in the dry white wine and cook for 2-3 minutes until it's mostly absorbed by the rice, stirring frequently.
7. Begin adding the warm broth to the skillet, one ladleful at a time, stirring constantly and allowing each addition to be absorbed before adding more. Continue this process until the rice is cooked through and creamy, about 45-50 minutes. You may not need to use all of the broth.
8. Once the rice is cooked to your desired consistency, stir in the grated Parmesan cheese until melted and creamy. Season with salt and pepper to taste.
9. Remove the skillet from the heat and let the risotto rest for a few minutes before serving.
10. Garnish the brown rice risotto with fresh herbs and additional Parmesan cheese if desired.
11. Serve the risotto hot as a main dish or side, and enjoy its creamy texture and nutty flavor!

This brown rice risotto is hearty, comforting, and packed with fiber and nutrients. It's a satisfying meal on its own or pairs well with roasted vegetables or grilled chicken for a complete and wholesome dinner.

Oven-Baked Chicken Wings

Ingredients:

- 2 pounds chicken wings, split at joints, tips removed
- 2 tablespoons olive oil
- 1 teaspoon garlic powder
- 1 teaspoon onion powder
- 1 teaspoon paprika
- 1/2 teaspoon salt
- 1/4 teaspoon black pepper
- Optional: your favorite hot sauce or BBQ sauce for serving

Instructions:

1. Preheat your oven to 425°F (220°C). Line a baking sheet with aluminum foil and place a wire rack on top.
2. In a large bowl, toss the chicken wings with olive oil until evenly coated.
3. In a small bowl, mix together the garlic powder, onion powder, paprika, salt, and black pepper.
4. Sprinkle the seasoning mixture over the chicken wings and toss until the wings are evenly coated with the seasoning.
5. Arrange the seasoned chicken wings in a single layer on the wire rack on the prepared baking sheet.
6. Bake the chicken wings in the preheated oven for 40-45 minutes, flipping halfway through, until they are golden brown and crispy.
7. Once the chicken wings are cooked through and crispy, remove them from the oven and let them cool for a few minutes before serving.
8. Serve the oven-baked chicken wings hot, either plain or with your favorite dipping sauce or hot sauce on the side.
9. Enjoy your crispy and flavorful oven-baked chicken wings as a tasty appetizer, snack, or main dish!

These oven-baked chicken wings are perfect for game day, parties, or any occasion where you're craving a delicious and satisfying snack. Plus, since they're baked instead of fried, they're a healthier option that doesn't sacrifice any flavor or crunchiness.

Spinach and Mushroom Quesadilla

Ingredients:

- 4 large flour tortillas
- 2 cups fresh spinach leaves, washed and chopped
- 1 cup mushrooms, sliced
- 1 small onion, thinly sliced
- 1 clove garlic, minced
- 1 cup shredded cheese (such as Monterey Jack, cheddar, or a Mexican cheese blend)
- 2 tablespoons olive oil
- Salt and pepper to taste
- Optional toppings: salsa, guacamole, sour cream, chopped cilantro

Instructions:

1. Heat 1 tablespoon of olive oil in a large skillet over medium heat. Add the sliced mushrooms and cook for 4-5 minutes until they start to brown and release their moisture. Remove the mushrooms from the skillet and set aside.
2. In the same skillet, add the remaining tablespoon of olive oil. Add the thinly sliced onion and minced garlic, and sauté for 2-3 minutes until the onion is translucent and fragrant.
3. Add the chopped spinach to the skillet and cook for 1-2 minutes until wilted. Season with salt and pepper to taste.
4. Place one flour tortilla on a clean surface. Spread a layer of the cooked spinach and onion mixture evenly over half of the tortilla.
5. Top the spinach mixture with some of the cooked mushrooms and a handful of shredded cheese.
6. Fold the empty half of the tortilla over the filling to create a half-moon shape.
7. Repeat the process with the remaining tortillas and filling ingredients.
8. Heat a large skillet or griddle over medium heat. Place the assembled quesadillas in the skillet and cook for 2-3 minutes on each side until golden brown and the cheese is melted.
9. Once cooked, remove the quesadillas from the skillet and let them cool for a minute before slicing them into wedges.
10. Serve the spinach and mushroom quesadillas hot, with your favorite toppings such as salsa, guacamole, sour cream, or chopped cilantro on the side.

These spinach and mushroom quesadillas are delicious, vegetarian-friendly, and packed with flavor. They make a perfect lunch, dinner, or appetizer for any occasion. Feel free to customize them by adding other ingredients like black beans, corn, or bell peppers to suit your taste preferences. Enjoy!

Roasted Brussels Sprouts

Ingredients:

- 1 pound Brussels sprouts
- 2 tablespoons olive oil
- Salt and pepper to taste
- Optional: grated Parmesan cheese, balsamic glaze, chopped bacon, or toasted nuts for garnish

Instructions:

1. Preheat your oven to 400°F (200°C). Line a baking sheet with parchment paper or aluminum foil for easy cleanup.
2. Trim the ends off the Brussels sprouts and remove any loose or discolored outer leaves. If the Brussels sprouts are large, you can cut them in half lengthwise for quicker and more even roasting.
3. Place the trimmed Brussels sprouts in a large mixing bowl. Drizzle them with olive oil and sprinkle with salt and pepper to taste. Toss the Brussels sprouts until they are evenly coated with the oil and seasoning.
4. Transfer the seasoned Brussels sprouts to the prepared baking sheet, spreading them out in a single layer.
5. Roast the Brussels sprouts in the preheated oven for 20-25 minutes, or until they are tender on the inside and caramelized and crispy on the outside. You can shake the pan or flip the Brussels sprouts halfway through cooking for even browning.
6. Once the Brussels sprouts are roasted to your desired level of doneness, remove them from the oven and transfer them to a serving dish.
7. If desired, garnish the roasted Brussels sprouts with grated Parmesan cheese, a drizzle of balsamic glaze, chopped cooked bacon, or toasted nuts before serving.
8. Serve the roasted Brussels sprouts hot as a side dish alongside your favorite main course.

These roasted Brussels sprouts are a versatile side dish that pairs well with a variety of flavors and cuisines. They're perfect for holiday dinners, weeknight meals, or any occasion when you want to add some delicious vegetables to your plate. Enjoy!

Eggplant Parmesan (baked)

Ingredients:

- 2 medium eggplants
- Salt
- 2 cups marinara sauce (store-bought or homemade)
- 2 cups shredded mozzarella cheese
- 1 cup grated Parmesan cheese
- 1 cup breadcrumbs (regular or panko)
- 1/4 cup chopped fresh basil or parsley (optional)
- Olive oil for brushing

Instructions:

1. Preheat your oven to 400°F (200°C). Line a baking sheet with parchment paper.
2. Slice the eggplants into 1/4-inch rounds. Place the slices in a colander and sprinkle them with salt. Let them sit for about 20 minutes to release excess moisture. Rinse the eggplant slices under cold water and pat them dry with paper towels.
3. Arrange the eggplant slices on the prepared baking sheet in a single layer. Brush both sides of the slices with olive oil.
4. In a shallow dish, combine the breadcrumbs with half of the grated Parmesan cheese. Dredge each eggplant slice in the breadcrumb mixture, coating both sides evenly. Place the coated slices back onto the baking sheet.
5. Bake the breaded eggplant slices in the preheated oven for 20-25 minutes, flipping halfway through, until golden brown and tender.
6. Remove the baked eggplant slices from the oven and reduce the oven temperature to 350°F (175°C).
7. Spread a thin layer of marinara sauce in the bottom of a baking dish. Arrange a layer of baked eggplant slices on top of the sauce. Sprinkle some shredded mozzarella cheese and grated Parmesan cheese over the eggplant slices. Repeat the layers until all the ingredients are used, ending with a layer of cheese on top.
8. Cover the baking dish with aluminum foil and bake in the oven for 20-25 minutes, until the cheese is melted and bubbly.
9. Remove the foil and bake for an additional 5-10 minutes, until the cheese is golden brown and the sauce is bubbly.
10. Remove the baked eggplant Parmesan from the oven and let it cool for a few minutes before serving. Garnish with chopped fresh basil or parsley, if desired.

11. Serve the baked eggplant Parmesan hot, with a side of pasta or a green salad, and enjoy!

This baked eggplant Parmesan is a healthier alternative to the traditional fried version, but it's just as delicious and satisfying. It's perfect for a comforting weeknight dinner or a special occasion meal.

Spaghetti Squash with Pesto

Ingredients:

- 1 medium spaghetti squash
- 2 tablespoons olive oil
- Salt and pepper to taste
- 1/2 cup pesto sauce (store-bought or homemade)
- Grated Parmesan cheese for serving (optional)
- Fresh basil leaves for garnish (optional)

Instructions:

1. Preheat your oven to 400°F (200°C). Line a baking sheet with parchment paper.
2. Cut the spaghetti squash in half lengthwise and scoop out the seeds and stringy pulp with a spoon.
3. Brush the cut sides of the spaghetti squash halves with olive oil and season with salt and pepper to taste.
4. Place the spaghetti squash halves, cut side down, on the prepared baking sheet.
5. Roast the spaghetti squash in the preheated oven for 35-45 minutes, or until the flesh is tender and easily pierced with a fork.
6. Once the spaghetti squash is cooked, remove it from the oven and let it cool for a few minutes.
7. Use a fork to scrape the flesh of the spaghetti squash into strands, resembling spaghetti noodles. Transfer the spaghetti squash strands to a serving dish.
8. Spoon the pesto sauce over the spaghetti squash strands and toss to coat evenly.
9. Serve the spaghetti squash with pesto hot, garnished with grated Parmesan cheese and fresh basil leaves, if desired.
10. Enjoy your delicious and nutritious spaghetti squash with pesto as a light and satisfying meal!

This dish is perfect for vegetarians and anyone looking for a gluten-free or low-carb alternative to traditional pasta dishes. It's packed with flavor from the homemade or store-bought pesto sauce and makes a great side dish or main course.

Avocado Toast

Ingredients:

- 1 ripe avocado
- 2 slices of your favorite bread (such as whole grain, sourdough, or gluten-free)
- Salt and pepper to taste
- Optional toppings: sliced cherry tomatoes, red pepper flakes, crushed red pepper, sesame seeds, everything bagel seasoning, crumbled feta cheese, sliced radishes, microgreens, poached or fried egg, smoked salmon, balsamic glaze, hot sauce, lime or lemon juice

Instructions:

1. Toast the slices of bread until golden brown and crispy.
2. While the bread is toasting, prepare the avocado. Cut the avocado in half lengthwise and remove the pit. Scoop the flesh into a bowl.
3. Use a fork to mash the avocado until smooth or leave it slightly chunky, depending on your preference. Season with salt and pepper to taste.
4. Once the toast is done, spread the mashed avocado evenly onto each slice of toast.
5. Top the avocado toast with your desired toppings. Get creative and mix and match different flavors and textures to suit your taste preferences.
6. Serve the avocado toast immediately, while the toast is still warm and crispy.
7. Enjoy your delicious and satisfying avocado toast for breakfast, brunch, or as a quick and healthy snack!

Avocado toast is versatile, nutritious, and can be customized in countless ways to suit your taste preferences and dietary needs. Whether you keep it simple with just avocado and salt or get creative with a variety of toppings, avocado toast is sure to be a hit any time of day.

Hearty Vegetable Stew

Ingredients:

- 2 tablespoons olive oil
- 1 onion, chopped
- 2 cloves garlic, minced
- 2 carrots, peeled and diced
- 2 celery stalks, diced
- 1 bell pepper, chopped
- 2 potatoes, peeled and diced
- 1 cup green beans, trimmed and cut into bite-sized pieces
- 1 can (14 oz) diced tomatoes
- 4 cups vegetable broth
- 1 teaspoon dried thyme
- 1 teaspoon dried rosemary
- Salt and pepper to taste
- 1 cup cooked chickpeas or white beans (optional)
- Chopped fresh parsley for garnish (optional)

Instructions:

1. Heat the olive oil in a large pot or Dutch oven over medium heat. Add the chopped onion and cook for 3-4 minutes until softened.
2. Add the minced garlic to the pot and cook for another minute until fragrant.
3. Add the diced carrots, celery, bell pepper, potatoes, and green beans to the pot. Stir to combine.
4. Pour in the diced tomatoes and vegetable broth. Stir in the dried thyme and rosemary. Season with salt and pepper to taste.
5. Bring the stew to a boil, then reduce the heat to low and let it simmer for 20-25 minutes, or until the vegetables are tender.
6. If using cooked chickpeas or white beans, stir them into the stew during the last 5 minutes of cooking to heat through.
7. Taste the stew and adjust the seasoning if needed.
8. Once the vegetables are tender and the stew is heated through, remove the pot from the heat.
9. Ladle the hearty vegetable stew into bowls and garnish with chopped fresh parsley, if desired.
10. Serve the stew hot, with crusty bread or rolls on the side for dipping and enjoy!

This hearty vegetable stew is packed with flavor and nutrients from a variety of colorful vegetables and herbs. It's a versatile dish that you can customize based on the vegetables you have on hand or your personal taste preferences. Plus, it's vegan and gluten-free, making it suitable for a wide range of dietary needs.

Banana Oatmeal Cookies

Ingredients:

- 2 ripe bananas, mashed
- 1 cup rolled oats (old-fashioned or quick oats)
- 1/4 cup almond butter or peanut butter
- 1/4 cup honey or maple syrup
- 1/2 teaspoon vanilla extract
- 1/2 teaspoon ground cinnamon
- 1/4 cup raisins, chocolate chips, chopped nuts, or dried fruit (optional)

Instructions:

1. Preheat your oven to 350°F (175°C). Line a baking sheet with parchment paper or lightly grease it with cooking spray.
2. In a large mixing bowl, combine the mashed bananas, rolled oats, almond butter or peanut butter, honey or maple syrup, vanilla extract, and ground cinnamon. Mix until all the ingredients are well combined and the mixture has a uniform consistency.
3. If using, fold in the optional add-ins such as raisins, chocolate chips, chopped nuts, or dried fruit until evenly distributed throughout the cookie dough.
4. Drop spoonfuls of the cookie dough onto the prepared baking sheet, spacing them about 2 inches apart. Use the back of a spoon or your fingers to flatten and shape the cookies into rounds, as they won't spread much during baking.
5. Bake the banana oatmeal cookies in the preheated oven for 12-15 minutes, or until the edges are golden brown and the cookies are set.
6. Once baked, remove the cookies from the oven and let them cool on the baking sheet for a few minutes before transferring them to a wire rack to cool completely.
7. Serve the banana oatmeal cookies as a wholesome snack or treat. Store any leftovers in an airtight container at room temperature for up to 3-4 days.

These banana oatmeal cookies are soft, chewy, and naturally sweetened with ripe bananas and honey or maple syrup. They're perfect for satisfying your sweet tooth while also providing a boost of energy from the oats and fruit. Enjoy them as a guilt-free treat any time of day!

Berry Smoothie Bowl

Ingredients:

For the smoothie:

- 1 cup mixed berries (such as strawberries, blueberries, raspberries, and blackberries), fresh or frozen
- 1 ripe banana, fresh or frozen
- 1/2 cup plain Greek yogurt or dairy-free yogurt
- 1/4 cup almond milk, coconut milk, or any milk of your choice
- 1 tablespoon honey or maple syrup (optional, depending on sweetness preference)
- 1 teaspoon vanilla extract (optional)

For the toppings:

- Fresh berries (such as sliced strawberries, blueberries, raspberries, and blackberries)
- Granola
- Sliced bananas
- Chia seeds
- Shredded coconut
- Nuts or seeds (such as almonds, walnuts, pumpkin seeds, or sunflower seeds)
- Honey or maple syrup for drizzling

Instructions:

1. In a blender, combine the mixed berries, banana, Greek yogurt, almond milk, honey or maple syrup (if using), and vanilla extract (if using). Blend until smooth and creamy. If the smoothie is too thick, add more almond milk, a splash at a time, until you reach your desired consistency.
2. Pour the berry smoothie into a bowl.
3. Arrange your desired toppings on top of the smoothie. Get creative and use a variety of toppings for texture and flavor.
4. Drizzle the smoothie bowl with honey or maple syrup for extra sweetness, if desired.
5. Serve the berry smoothie bowl immediately and enjoy it with a spoon!

This berry smoothie bowl is not only delicious but also customizable based on your preferences and dietary needs. It's a great way to start your day with a nutritious and filling breakfast or to enjoy as a refreshing snack any time of day. Feel free to experiment with different combinations of fruits, yogurt, and toppings to create your perfect smoothie bowl!

Lemon Herb Grilled Chicken

Ingredients:

- 4 boneless, skinless chicken breasts
- 1/4 cup olive oil
- Zest and juice of 1 lemon
- 2 cloves garlic, minced
- 2 tablespoons chopped fresh herbs (such as parsley, thyme, rosemary, or basil)
- 1 teaspoon dried oregano
- 1 teaspoon dried thyme
- Salt and pepper to taste

Instructions:

1. In a small bowl, whisk together the olive oil, lemon zest, lemon juice, minced garlic, chopped fresh herbs, dried oregano, dried thyme, salt, and pepper to make the marinade.
2. Place the chicken breasts in a shallow dish or a large resealable plastic bag.
3. Pour the marinade over the chicken breasts, making sure they are evenly coated. Massage the marinade into the chicken to ensure it's well distributed. Cover the dish or seal the bag, and refrigerate for at least 30 minutes or up to 4 hours to allow the flavors to meld and the chicken to marinate.
4. Preheat your grill to medium-high heat. Make sure the grill grates are clean and lightly oiled to prevent sticking.
5. Remove the chicken breasts from the marinade and discard any excess marinade.
6. Place the chicken breasts on the preheated grill and cook for 6-8 minutes per side, or until the chicken is cooked through and no longer pink in the center. The internal temperature of the chicken should reach 165°F (75°C) when measured with a meat thermometer.
7. Once cooked, remove the chicken breasts from the grill and let them rest for a few minutes before serving to allow the juices to redistribute.
8. Serve the lemon herb grilled chicken hot, garnished with additional fresh herbs or lemon slices if desired.

This lemon herb grilled chicken is delicious served with your favorite sides, such as grilled vegetables, rice, or a fresh salad. It's versatile, flavorful, and sure to be a hit at your next cookout or family dinner!

Chickpea Salad

Ingredients:

- 2 cans (15 oz each) chickpeas (garbanzo beans), drained and rinsed
- 1 red bell pepper, diced
- 1 cucumber, diced
- 1/2 red onion, finely chopped
- 1/4 cup chopped fresh parsley or cilantro
- 1/4 cup crumbled feta cheese (optional)
- 1/4 cup sliced Kalamata olives (optional)
- Salt and pepper to taste

For the dressing:

- 1/4 cup extra virgin olive oil
- 2 tablespoons lemon juice (about 1 lemon)
- 1 clove garlic, minced
- 1 teaspoon Dijon mustard
- 1 teaspoon honey or maple syrup
- Salt and pepper to taste

Instructions:

1. In a large mixing bowl, combine the drained and rinsed chickpeas, diced red bell pepper, diced cucumber, finely chopped red onion, chopped fresh parsley or cilantro, crumbled feta cheese (if using), and sliced Kalamata olives (if using). Toss gently to combine.
2. In a small bowl, whisk together the extra virgin olive oil, lemon juice, minced garlic, Dijon mustard, honey or maple syrup, salt, and pepper to make the dressing.
3. Pour the dressing over the chickpea salad and toss until everything is evenly coated.
4. Taste the chickpea salad and adjust the seasoning with additional salt and pepper if needed.
5. Cover the bowl with plastic wrap or transfer the salad to an airtight container and refrigerate for at least 30 minutes to allow the flavors to meld together.
6. Once chilled, give the chickpea salad a final toss and serve it cold as a light and refreshing meal or side dish.
7. Enjoy your delicious and nutritious chickpea salad!

This chickpea salad is versatile and can be customized with your favorite vegetables, herbs, and toppings. It's packed with protein, fiber, and vitamins, making it a healthy and satisfying option for any occasion. Feel free to experiment with different ingredients to create your own unique version of this tasty salad!

Roasted Beet Salad

Ingredients:

For the roasted beets:

- 4 medium-sized beets, washed and trimmed
- 2 tablespoons olive oil
- Salt and pepper to taste

For the salad:

- 6 cups mixed salad greens (such as spinach, arugula, or mesclun)
- 1/2 cup crumbled goat cheese or feta cheese
- 1/4 cup chopped walnuts, pecans, or almonds
- 1/4 cup dried cranberries or pomegranate seeds
- Balsamic glaze or vinaigrette dressing for drizzling (optional)

Instructions:

1. Preheat your oven to 400°F (200°C). Line a baking sheet with parchment paper.
2. Place the washed and trimmed beets on the prepared baking sheet. Drizzle them with olive oil and sprinkle with salt and pepper to taste. Toss to coat evenly.
3. Roast the beets in the preheated oven for 45-60 minutes, or until they are tender when pierced with a fork. The roasting time will depend on the size of the beets. Once roasted, remove the beets from the oven and let them cool slightly.
4. Once the roasted beets are cool enough to handle, peel off the skins using your fingers or a small knife. Cut the beets into bite-sized wedges or slices.
5. In a large salad bowl, combine the mixed salad greens with the roasted beet wedges.
6. Sprinkle the crumbled goat cheese or feta cheese, chopped nuts, and dried cranberries or pomegranate seeds over the salad greens and beets.
7. Drizzle the salad with balsamic glaze or vinaigrette dressing, if using, for added flavor. Alternatively, you can serve the dressing on the side for individual drizzling.
8. Toss the salad gently to combine all the ingredients.
9. Serve the roasted beet salad immediately as a side dish or light meal.
10. Enjoy your colorful and flavorful roasted beet salad!

This roasted beet salad is a perfect balance of sweet, savory, and tangy flavors, with a delightful combination of textures. It's a versatile dish that can be served as a starter, side dish, or main course, and it's sure to impress your family and friends with its beautiful presentation and delicious taste.

Stuffed Bell Peppers

Ingredients:

- 4 large bell peppers (any color), tops removed and seeds removed
- 1 tablespoon olive oil
- 1 small onion, finely chopped
- 2 cloves garlic, minced
- 1 pound ground beef, turkey, or chicken (or use cooked quinoa or lentils for a vegetarian option)
- 1 cup cooked rice (white, brown, or wild rice)
- 1 can (14 oz) diced tomatoes, drained
- 1 teaspoon dried oregano
- 1 teaspoon dried basil
- Salt and pepper to taste
- 1 cup shredded cheese (such as cheddar, mozzarella, or Monterey Jack), divided
- Chopped fresh parsley or cilantro for garnish (optional)

Instructions:

1. Preheat your oven to 375°F (190°C). Lightly grease a baking dish large enough to hold the bell peppers upright.
2. Heat the olive oil in a large skillet over medium heat. Add the chopped onion and minced garlic, and sauté for 2-3 minutes until softened and fragrant.
3. Add the ground meat (or cooked quinoa or lentils) to the skillet, breaking it up with a spoon, and cook until browned and cooked through.
4. Stir in the cooked rice, diced tomatoes, dried oregano, dried basil, salt, and pepper. Cook for another 2-3 minutes to allow the flavors to meld together.
5. Remove the skillet from the heat and stir in 1/2 cup of shredded cheese until melted and well combined.
6. Stuff each bell pepper with the meat and rice mixture, pressing down gently to fill the peppers evenly. Place the stuffed peppers upright in the prepared baking dish.
7. Sprinkle the remaining 1/2 cup of shredded cheese evenly over the tops of the stuffed peppers.
8. Cover the baking dish with aluminum foil and bake in the preheated oven for 25-30 minutes, or until the peppers are tender and the filling is heated through.
9. Remove the foil and bake for an additional 5-10 minutes, or until the cheese is melted and bubbly and the tops of the peppers are lightly golden brown.

10. Remove the stuffed bell peppers from the oven and let them cool for a few minutes before serving.
11. Garnish the stuffed bell peppers with chopped fresh parsley or cilantro, if desired, and serve hot.

These stuffed bell peppers are a satisfying and comforting meal that's perfect for any occasion. You can customize the filling with your favorite ingredients and spices to suit your taste preferences, making them a versatile dish that's sure to please everyone at the table. Enjoy!

Carrot and Zucchini Muffins

Ingredients:

- 1 cup all-purpose flour
- 1/2 cup whole wheat flour
- 1/2 cup rolled oats
- 1 teaspoon baking powder
- 1/2 teaspoon baking soda
- 1/2 teaspoon salt
- 1 teaspoon ground cinnamon
- 1/4 teaspoon ground nutmeg
- 2 large eggs
- 1/2 cup brown sugar or coconut sugar
- 1/2 cup unsweetened applesauce
- 1/4 cup olive oil or melted coconut oil
- 1 teaspoon vanilla extract
- 1 cup grated carrot (about 2 medium carrots)
- 1 cup grated zucchini (about 1 medium zucchini)
- 1/2 cup chopped nuts or seeds (such as walnuts, pecans, or pumpkin seeds) (optional)

Instructions:

1. Preheat your oven to 350°F (175°C). Line a muffin tin with paper liners or grease the muffin cups with cooking spray.
2. In a large mixing bowl, whisk together the all-purpose flour, whole wheat flour, rolled oats, baking powder, baking soda, salt, ground cinnamon, and ground nutmeg until well combined.
3. In a separate bowl, beat the eggs with the brown sugar or coconut sugar until smooth and creamy.
4. Stir in the unsweetened applesauce, olive oil or melted coconut oil, and vanilla extract until well combined.
5. Gradually add the wet ingredients to the dry ingredients, mixing until just combined. Be careful not to overmix.
6. Fold in the grated carrot, grated zucchini, and chopped nuts or seeds (if using) until evenly distributed throughout the batter.
7. Divide the batter evenly among the prepared muffin cups, filling each about 2/3 full.

8. Bake the muffins in the preheated oven for 18-20 minutes, or until a toothpick inserted into the center of a muffin comes out clean.
9. Once baked, remove the muffins from the oven and let them cool in the muffin tin for a few minutes before transferring them to a wire rack to cool completely.
10. Serve the carrot and zucchini muffins warm or at room temperature, and enjoy!

These carrot and zucchini muffins are moist, flavorful, and packed with fiber and nutrients from the carrots and zucchini. They're a great way to sneak some extra veggies into your diet, and they're sure to be a hit with kids and adults alike. Enjoy them for breakfast, as a snack, or as a wholesome treat any time of day!

Hummus and Veggie Wrap

Ingredients:

- 1 large whole wheat or spinach tortilla
- 1/4 cup hummus (store-bought or homemade)
- 1/2 cup mixed salad greens (such as lettuce, spinach, or arugula)
- 1/4 cup shredded carrots
- 1/4 cup thinly sliced cucumber
- 1/4 cup sliced bell peppers (any color)
- 1/4 cup sliced avocado
- 2-3 tablespoons crumbled feta cheese or shredded cheese (optional)
- Salt and pepper to taste

Instructions:

1. Lay the whole wheat or spinach tortilla flat on a clean surface.
2. Spread the hummus evenly over the surface of the tortilla, leaving a small border around the edges.
3. Layer the mixed salad greens, shredded carrots, thinly sliced cucumber, sliced bell peppers, sliced avocado, and crumbled feta cheese or shredded cheese (if using) on top of the hummus.
4. Season the veggies with salt and pepper to taste.
5. Fold in the sides of the tortilla, then roll it up tightly from the bottom to enclose the filling, forming a wrap.
6. Slice the hummus and veggie wrap in half diagonally with a sharp knife.
7. Serve the wrap immediately, or wrap it tightly in plastic wrap or aluminum foil for later enjoyment.
8. Enjoy your delicious and satisfying hummus and veggie wrap!

This hummus and veggie wrap is packed with fiber, vitamins, and minerals from the colorful assortment of vegetables, and the hummus adds a creamy and flavorful touch. It's a great option for a healthy lunch or snack that's both filling and satisfying. Feel free to customize the wrap with your favorite veggies, cheese, or spreads to suit your taste preferences.

Grilled Asparagus

Ingredients:

- 1 bunch of fresh asparagus
- 2 tablespoons olive oil
- Salt and pepper to taste
- Optional toppings: grated Parmesan cheese, lemon zest, balsamic glaze, chopped fresh herbs (such as parsley or thyme)

Instructions:

1. Preheat your grill to medium-high heat.
2. Wash the asparagus and trim off the woody ends.
3. In a shallow dish or bowl, toss the asparagus spears with olive oil until evenly coated. Season with salt and pepper to taste.
4. Place the asparagus spears directly on the preheated grill grate, perpendicular to the grill grates (this prevents them from falling through). Alternatively, you can use a grill basket or place them on a sheet of aluminum foil.
5. Grill the asparagus for 5-7 minutes, turning occasionally with tongs, until they are tender and lightly charred. The cooking time may vary depending on the thickness of the asparagus spears and the heat of your grill.
6. Once cooked, remove the grilled asparagus from the grill and transfer them to a serving platter.
7. If desired, sprinkle the grilled asparagus with grated Parmesan cheese, lemon zest, balsamic glaze, or chopped fresh herbs for added flavor.
8. Serve the grilled asparagus hot as a side dish alongside your favorite main course.

Grilled asparagus is a simple yet elegant side dish that's perfect for summer cookouts, BBQs, or weeknight dinners. It's quick to prepare, packed with flavor, and adds a nutritious touch to any meal. Enjoy!

Tomato Basil Soup

Ingredients:

- 2 tablespoons olive oil
- 1 onion, chopped
- 2 cloves garlic, minced
- 2 cans (14 oz each) diced tomatoes
- 1 can (14 oz) tomato sauce
- 2 cups vegetable broth
- 1 teaspoon dried basil
- 1/2 teaspoon dried oregano
- Salt and pepper to taste
- 1/2 cup heavy cream or coconut cream (optional)
- Fresh basil leaves for garnish (optional)

Instructions:

1. In a large pot or Dutch oven, heat the olive oil over medium heat. Add the chopped onion and cook for 3-4 minutes until softened.
2. Add the minced garlic to the pot and cook for another minute until fragrant.
3. Stir in the diced tomatoes (with their juices), tomato sauce, vegetable broth, dried basil, and dried oregano. Season with salt and pepper to taste.
4. Bring the soup to a simmer, then reduce the heat to low. Cover and let the soup simmer for 15-20 minutes to allow the flavors to meld together.
5. Once the soup has simmered, use an immersion blender to puree the soup until smooth. Alternatively, you can transfer the soup in batches to a blender and blend until smooth, then return it to the pot.
6. If using heavy cream or coconut cream, stir it into the soup until well combined. This step is optional but adds creaminess to the soup.
7. Taste the soup and adjust the seasoning if needed. If the soup is too thick, you can add more vegetable broth or water to reach your desired consistency.
8. Ladle the tomato basil soup into bowls and garnish with fresh basil leaves, if desired.
9. Serve the soup hot with crusty bread or grilled cheese sandwiches on the side, and enjoy!

This tomato basil soup is rich, creamy, and bursting with the flavors of ripe tomatoes and fragrant basil. It's a comforting and satisfying meal that's perfect for a chilly day or any time you're craving a bowl of soup. Plus, it's easy to make and can be ready in under 30 minutes!

Chicken Caesar Salad (lightened)

Ingredients:

For the chicken:

- 2 boneless, skinless chicken breasts
- 1 tablespoon olive oil
- Salt and pepper to taste
- 1 teaspoon garlic powder
- 1 teaspoon dried Italian herbs (such as basil, oregano, thyme)

For the salad:

- 1 large head of romaine lettuce, washed and chopped
- 1/4 cup grated Parmesan cheese
- Whole grain croutons (store-bought or homemade)
- Optional: cherry tomatoes, cucumber slices, red onion slices

For the dressing:

- 1/4 cup plain Greek yogurt
- 2 tablespoons grated Parmesan cheese
- 1 tablespoon lemon juice
- 1 teaspoon Dijon mustard
- 1 clove garlic, minced
- Salt and pepper to taste
- Water, to thin the dressing if necessary

Instructions:

1. Preheat your oven to 375°F (190°C). Line a baking sheet with parchment paper.
2. Rub the chicken breasts with olive oil and season them with salt, pepper, garlic powder, and dried Italian herbs.
3. Place the seasoned chicken breasts on the prepared baking sheet and bake in the preheated oven for 20-25 minutes, or until cooked through and no longer pink in the center. Once cooked, remove the chicken from the oven and let it cool slightly before slicing it into strips.
4. While the chicken is cooking, prepare the salad ingredients. In a large bowl, combine the chopped romaine lettuce, grated Parmesan cheese, whole grain croutons, and any optional salad toppings you like.

5. In a small bowl, whisk together the plain Greek yogurt, grated Parmesan cheese, lemon juice, Dijon mustard, minced garlic, salt, and pepper to make the dressing. If the dressing is too thick, you can thin it out with a little water until you reach your desired consistency.
6. Add the sliced chicken breast to the salad bowl, then drizzle the dressing over the top.
7. Toss the salad gently until everything is evenly coated with the dressing.
8. Serve the chicken Caesar salad immediately, and enjoy!

This lightened-up version of chicken Caesar salad is still packed with flavor and protein from the grilled chicken, while the Greek yogurt-based dressing provides creaminess without all the calories of a traditional Caesar dressing. It's a nutritious and satisfying meal that's perfect for lunch or dinner. Feel free to customize the salad with your favorite toppings and enjoy!

Sweet Potato and Kale Hash

Ingredients:

- 2 medium sweet potatoes, peeled and diced into small cubes
- 1 tablespoon olive oil
- 1 small onion, diced
- 2 cloves garlic, minced
- 4 cups chopped kale leaves, tough stems removed
- Salt and pepper to taste
- Optional toppings: fried or poached eggs, avocado slices, chopped green onions, hot sauce

Instructions:

1. Heat the olive oil in a large skillet over medium heat. Add the diced sweet potatoes to the skillet and cook, stirring occasionally, for about 5 minutes until they start to soften.
2. Add the diced onion to the skillet and cook for another 3-4 minutes until the onion is translucent and the sweet potatoes are tender.
3. Stir in the minced garlic and cook for another minute until fragrant.
4. Add the chopped kale leaves to the skillet and cook, stirring occasionally, for 3-4 minutes until the kale is wilted and tender. Season with salt and pepper to taste.
5. Once the sweet potatoes are cooked through and the kale is wilted, remove the skillet from the heat.
6. Serve the sweet potato and kale hash hot, either on its own or topped with fried or poached eggs, avocado slices, chopped green onions, and hot sauce if desired.
7. Enjoy your delicious and nutritious sweet potato and kale hash!

This sweet potato and kale hash is a satisfying and versatile dish that's packed with flavor and nutrients. It's perfect for a hearty breakfast or brunch, but you can also enjoy it as a side dish or even a light dinner. Feel free to customize the hash with your favorite seasonings or add-ins to suit your taste preferences.

Blueberry Chia Pudding

Ingredients:

- 1 cup unsweetened almond milk or any milk of your choice
- 1/4 cup chia seeds
- 1 tablespoon maple syrup or honey (optional, adjust to taste)
- 1/2 teaspoon vanilla extract
- 1/2 cup fresh or frozen blueberries
- Additional toppings: fresh blueberries, sliced almonds, shredded coconut, granola

Instructions:

1. In a mixing bowl or jar, combine the unsweetened almond milk, chia seeds, maple syrup or honey (if using), and vanilla extract. Stir well to combine.
2. Gently fold in the fresh or frozen blueberries until evenly distributed throughout the mixture.
3. Cover the bowl or jar and refrigerate the blueberry chia pudding for at least 2-3 hours, or preferably overnight, to allow the chia seeds to absorb the liquid and thicken the pudding.
4. Once the chia pudding has set and thickened to your desired consistency, give it a good stir to redistribute the ingredients.
5. Divide the blueberry chia pudding into serving bowls or jars.
6. Top the pudding with additional fresh blueberries, sliced almonds, shredded coconut, granola, or any other toppings of your choice.
7. Serve the blueberry chia pudding cold and enjoy it as a nutritious breakfast, snack, or dessert!

This blueberry chia pudding is not only delicious but also versatile and customizable. You can adjust the sweetness level by adding more or less maple syrup or honey, and you can also experiment with different toppings to suit your taste preferences. Plus, it's vegan, gluten-free, and dairy-free, making it suitable for a wide range of dietary preferences.

www.ingramcontent.com/pod-product-compliance
Lightning Source LLC
LaVergne TN
LVHW081613060526
838201LV00054B/2228